# Contents

Expert tips for Minecraft Story Mode Season Two!

Find out what to do when the Zombies are after you!

# Inside...

# Build It!

# GIANT BUNNY

## Have a go at building a giant Bunny for you to live inside!

**10 MINUTES!**

**START HERE!**

**1** YOU start your giant bunny by making a rectangle on stilts out of White Wool that is 7 blocks wide and 10 blocks deep, with 2 blocks high stilts supporting it. Build up 4 blocks of White Wool on each corner, then join the corners together to make another 7x10 block rectangle on top.

**2** NOW fill in all of the empty space in your frame with White Wool, even the floor and the roof. Decide which end will be his face, then build out left and right to make his front legs 2x2x4 White Wool blocks. For the back legs, copy the pattern above on both left and right sides.

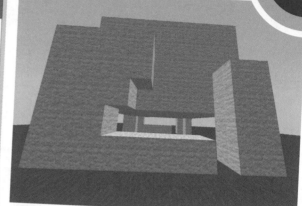

**3** THE back legs underneath the bunny are 2 blocks wide, so add more White Wool to fill them out, also build out the back legs 1 block back and 1 block to the side so they stick out slightly. Then between his back legs you need a square 3x3 of White Wool to make his tail, with a Light Grey Wool block in the centre.

**BUILD THIS!**

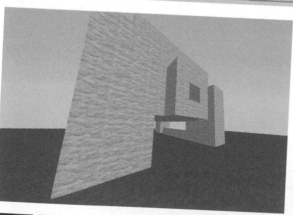

**4** YOUR bunny needs a head! It's a 5x4x5 White Wool box, set 2 blocks into the bunny's body. For finishing touches add a Pink Wool block nose 3 blocks down in the centre of his head, add two 2 Red Wool block high eyes either side of his nose and two floppy ears. To make the ears use a 5x2 White Wool rectangle on each side, with a 4x1 inner in Pink Wool.

WHAT DO YOU CALL A RABBIT WITH FLEAS? BUGS BUNNY!

# KNOW YOUR MINECRAFT MOBS!

*One of the joys of Minecraft is the amazing collection of MOBs you can encounter. Here's a closer look at the scary Ender Dragon!*

**THE ENDER DRAGON** was the first boss ever to be added to Minecraft! It is a giant flying black dragon found at the end of... The End. When you enter The End the Ender Dragon will spawn, no matter which difficulty level you are on – even Peaceful. If you are playing in Peaceful mode though, the Ender Dragon will not be able to directly hurt you. Be careful though, you can still be hurt by its fireballs!

**THIS GIANT** dragon has four moves you need to be aware of. It starts out circling around the ring of pillars looking for End Crystals. With the crystals gone it will start strafing around – firing its fireballs at you if you are within a 64 block radius. When it spies you it will dive directly at your position – run! After diving the dragon will go back to circling around again. When it's a bit tired it will perch on top of an empty portal.

**WHEN YOU** have defeated the Ender Dragon it will slowly come down to the ground, looking a bit tattered and torn. Beams of light will explode from its body – you did that! Enjoy your 12,000 experience points. If you miss the Ender Dragon you can always spawn it again in your game by placing four End Crystals on top of an Exit Portal. It needs to be one on each side.

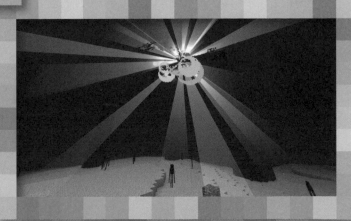

## BED WARS

**WHAT IS IT?** This is a team survival game on the Hypixel network based around protecting your bed from the enemy and breaking other team's beds as quickly as you can. It's a bit like a 'Capture The Flag' game, but with beds instead of flags!

**HOW DO I WIN?** You first need to stand in your island's Iron and Gold Generator to gather lots of resources which you can trade with Villagers for various items that will help you in your battle. You win by killing everyone else, and destroying their beds so they can't respawn.

**EXPERT TIPS!** Build to the Diamond and Emerald Generators in the centre of the map to obtain better items. Create a protective layer around your bed with any hard blocks that are difficult to destroy, and if you can, use Water and Ladders in your bed defences to make life harder for your enemies.

**DID YOU KNOW?** Bed Wars is now an official game on the Hypixel Network. You can trade Bed Wars coins in exchange for a variety of celebrations that trigger when you win – our favourites are the fireworks and love hearts that shoot into the air.

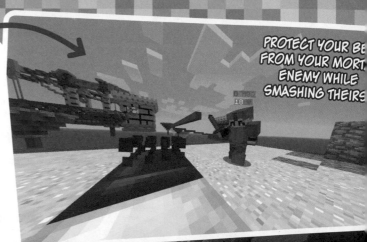

PROTECT YOUR BED FROM YOUR MORTAL ENEMY WHILE SMASHING THEIRS

# MULTIPLAYER GAME TIPS

*Quick tips and hints to improve your PvP gaming!*

USE BLOCKS TO BUILD PATHWAYS TO THE CENTRE OF THE MAP – THAT'S WHERE THE GOOD STUFF IS!

## SKY WARS

**WHAT IS IT?** Everyone in the game has their own pre-built island with 3 Chests on it full of all kinds of goodies to pick up. The key to winning the game is to build to the centre of the map where there are more Chests with better gear. You need to give yourself an advantage.

**HOW DO I WIN?** This is a game of 'Last Man Standing' – so you just have to kill everyone else on the map before they kill you! It's very easy to lose your footing and fall off the map into the void. Once you have obtained the good gear in the centre you must go around and pick off each target one by one.

**EXPERT TIPS!** Use Snowballs and Eggs as a cheaper substitute to Bows and Arrows in your battles. They have the same knockback rating as Arrows, but are much more common and can be thrown instantly. This will make it easier to knock people off into the void while they are trying to cross to different islands.

**DID YOU KNOW?** Sky Wars is officialy the most popular PvP game on the Hypixel Network. We have often seen over 15,000 players battling it out on the server at the same time. Woah!

# TURBO KART RACERS

**WHAT IS IT?** You've played Mario Kart right? This is Hypixel's own take on the go-karting game. Turbo Kart Racers is a fast paced action racer where you must complete the track 3 times while avoiding other player's traps and getting them with your own.

**HOW DO I WIN?** With clever use of traps and speed boosts, you must push yourself out front and be in first position when crossing the finish line after 3 laps. By looking at the data on the right of the screen while playing you can see the position you are in and what lap you are on.

**EXPERT TIPS!** Familiarise yourself with the pre-made tracks, there are some shortcuts you can search out that will save you lots of time and push you into the lead. Drive through the spinning "?" blocks to obtain a random power-up. Mushroom Boosters are the best – they give you a big speed boost.

**DID YOU KNOW?** You can customise your helmet, your go-kart and even your horn sound in the game. You do this by buying them in the TKR store for coins that you pick up for free while racing around the track.

# JOINING IN...

**THESE FOUR GAMES** come from the PvP (Player Vs Player) server Hypixel. We have chosen this one as it's about the most child-friendly of them all, and you can join in without having to pay anything. When you start Minecraft, click Multiplayer then Add Server. Name the server 'Hypixel' and in the address bar below enter hypixel.net. Click Add Server then when you are back at the server list screen, click on Join Server to enter Hypixel. Walk around to find the games!

*OOO... A ? BLOCK! I HOPE THERE'S A MUSHROOM BOOSTER INSIDE!*

# BUILD BATTLE

**WHAT IS IT?** No swords, battling or smashing people here – this is a timed challenge game where you are asked to build something in 4 minutes. The twist is that everyone else playing is also building the same thing! At the end of the game you get to rate each other's handiwork.

**HOW DO I WIN?** You win by adding lots of detail to your build that others might not bother with. You want your build to stand out and look a bit special. Something that will make others want to give you a high rating. Once the 4 minutes building time is over you are teleported to everybody else's plot to rate them from Super Poop to Legendary!

**EXPERT TIPS!** By clicking the Netherstar in your 9th Hotbar slot you can spawn-in many character heads, customised banners, particle effects and even Mobs to improve your build. You can also change the time of day and the weather to fit the theme and give your build the wow factor!

**DID YOU KNOW?** Players with a YouTube rank get to decide on the themes for builds, and you can even have teams of two, working together!

*WHAT DO YOU THINK OF OUR PYRAMID? NOT TOO SHABBY, EH?*

**60 MINUTES!**

# SUSPENSION BRIDGE

## Just like the Golden Gate Bridge... only smaller!

**DIFFICULTY**

**NORMAL**
WHILE THE BRIDGE IS BIG, IT'S NOT TOO TRICKY TO BUILD

**START HERE!**

**1** SO YOU have a large span of area between two areas of land – how on Earth are you going to get across that without taking a swim? You need a Suspension Bridge! Start by building a flat road of Red Stained Clay blocks, 9 blocks wide and as long as you need to 'bridge' your gap.

**2** A BORING flat road isn't what you want. Make an archway on both sides of your bridge, far enough away from the land so that its foundations can be placed in the sea. Make it 1 block in from the edge of the road, 8 blocks up and 7 blocks across. Be sure to make both arches in the same way.

**3** CONTINUE TO build up from your first archway, giving it a 3 block thickness between the three holes (as seen in the picture). We have added extra blocks in the corners to give the holes a circular look. The total height of your bridge pillar should be 42 blocks. Repeat the other side.

**4** YOUR BRIDGE now needs cables to hold the large pillars in place in high winds. Start building up from the end of the roadway using Stone Bricks and Stone Stairs, we added extra Oak Fence blocks underneath ours. Try to build the cables in a curve, leading up to the high point on your pillar.

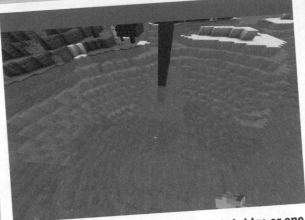

**5** REPEAT THE cables on the other side of your bridge, trying to be symmetrical. The **Oak Fence** pieces underneath the **Stone Stair** cables will also help when we come to adding in horizontal cables. Next, curve the cables down from each pillar into a semi-circle shape, meeting **28 blocks** from the road surface in the centre of the bridge.

**6** NOW WE need to strengthen this bridge or one gust of wind and it's going to fall into the sea. Build down from the road with **Red Stained Clay** blocks, ending just under the water surface. Now build a large **7x13 Stone Brick** block attached to the bedrock. Use Night Vision to see better underwater.

**7** SO YOU have **Stone Brick** cables hanging in the air from your pillars. If you have done bridges at school you will know about the forces that need to be sent through the bridge. Add **Oak Fence** cables every **5 blocks**, running vertical and attaching to the road surface far below.

**8** WITH THE bridge complete, you can now decide how you want to travel across. Why not try building a car? Although that's going nowhere. What we did was add a **Powered Rail** all the way along the bridge and popped a **Minecart** on there. Jumping into the cart and pressing Up you can zip along the bridge at quite a speed! Try it for yourself.

**BUILD THIS!**

**9** WE THINK our finished Suspension Bridge looks a bit like the Golden Gate Bridge in San Francisco, USA. But you can customise your bridge however you wish. Try different materials like Iron Bars instead of the Oak Fence, or maybe add a boat sailing underneath the bridge? Happy building!

WOW! I WOULD LOVE TO DO A BUNGIE JUMP FROM THE TOP OF THAT BRIDGE!

# Build It!

# MEGA LIVING ROOM!

## With TV, sofa, bookshelf and laptop – luxury!

**60 MINUTES!**

**NORMAL**
MAKING A GOOD LOOKING ROOM
IS ALL ABOUT THE DETAIL

**START HERE!**

**1** **LET'S BEGIN** our mega living room build by dropping down a row of 4 Wood blocks against a wall. From here add buttons to the 2 middle blocks to turn it into a cupboard, then place 2 Black Wool blocks directly above followed by a 4x3 rectangle above the 2 Wool blocks.

**2** **ALL THAT'S** left now to create the centrepiece of your living room is to place a giant Painting on the Black Wool rectangle we just made. Then add buttons on the right hand side. There you go! You've now got a flatscreen TV and a TV cabinet! Now, can it pick up the Disney channel?

**3** **IN FRONT** of the giant television you just built, dig up a 5x5 block section and cover it in Acacia Wood blocks. This area is going to be for our sofa so we can watch TV while chilling out with our friends. We won't be ordering from Ikea though – we're going to build it ourselves!

L2 Place    R2 Mine

**4** **PLACE A** row of Sandstone block steps along two of the sides. Make sure to leave a gap in the corner and at one of the ends. Fill in the corner gap, then place a step facing out on the furthest right side. Finally, add a step poking out on the left and your massive sofa is complete.

**5** WHAT'S A living room without a stereo? To create a high-tech stereo system simply place **2 Jukeboxes** on top of each other with a **2-high** set of Bedrock either side. Place an **Item Frame** on each of the **Bedrock** speakers then finish by adding another set of **Bedrock** to each **Frame** and spinning them once.

**6** GRAB SOME **Bookshelf** blocks and make a **3-high stack**. Count 3 blocks to the right and on the fourth, make another 3-high stack of **Books**. After that, fill in the top of the bookshelf with **Wood Slabs**. In between the shelves create an 'n' shape out of **Stone Slabs** to create the desk.

**7** FOR THE laptop, place a **Stone Pressure Plate** on the desk with a block behind it. Add a **Painting** of your choice for the screen. To make the chair, drop another **Stone Slab** on the floor surrounded by a **Wooden Trapdoor** then activate each of them to form the sides.

**8** TO FINISH off our living room properly all we need is a cool dining table big enough for the whole family. Dig up a **2-deep, 4x4 hole**. Fill the bottom of the hole with **Redstone** blocks. Around the inside of the hole, while looking down into it, place **Pistons** so that they automatically extend.

**BUILD THIS!**

**9** AND LAST but not least, add some **Black Carpet** on top of the **Pistons** (and in the middle of the hole), then in the 2x2 gaps, place some **Glass** blocks. Finish up by adding **Quartz** steps around the table and your swanky new living room is complete. Just in time to enjoy the new episode of The Flash!

LOOKS LIKE THE KIND OF PLACE I COULD CALL HOME!

# PUZZLES

## Test your brains with this teaser...

DOWN AT THE BOTTOM OF THE DEEP BLUE SEA...

## SPOT THE DIFFERENCE

**TO CELEBRATE** the release of the new Minecraft Aquatic update, we have gone and made 10 changes to this brilliant Aquatic scene for you to spot. Mark all the ones you can find on picture 2!

**PICTURE 1**

**PICTURE 2**

HOW MANY DIFFERENCES CAN YOU SPOT IN PICTURE 2?

ANSWERS ON PAGE 48

10

# KNOW YOUR MINECRAFT MOBS!

It's the MOBs in Minecraft that make the game so much fun to play! Here are our expert tips on what you can do with the Minecraft Pigs

THE LITTLE Pigs in Minecraft are some of the cutest MOBs you will find. Not only are they pink and friendly, but you can ride them too! Place a Saddle on their back and dangle a Carrot on a Stick in front of them and off you go! They spawn on grass blocks, and herds of Pigs appear on the generation of a new world. There's a 5% chance that a Pig will be a Baby Pig when spawning!

PIGS ARE not as stupid as they first seem! They might just wander around your world, bumping into each other, but they are not daft enough to fall off cliffs, into water or lava. They will follow you if you are carrying a Carrot, Potato or Beetroot, but get too far away (about eight blocks) and they will lose interest in you. If there's lightning around, be careful – a Pig struck by lightning becomes a Zombie Pigman!

THERE IS so much fun to be had with Pigs! If you are riding one and use the Invisibility status effect on it, the Pig becomes invisible, but not the Saddle! Riding on a Pig inside a Minecart will boost the speed the Minecart travels! Then, sadly, we come to the killing of pigs: a grown up Pig will drop 1-3 Raw Porkchops when killed, the Porkchops will be cooked if they are killed with fire!

# THE SECRETS OF...
# WORLD OF

Released in the Summer of 2017, the World of Colour update to Minecraft was packed with fun new features to enjoy...

This works on...
☒ Computer Edition

### SAY HELLO TO THE ILLUSIONER

**1** **THIS CHAP** has been hidden away inside Minecraft for a while – he's one of the Illagers (not to be confused with Villagers), along with the Vindicator and Evoker. It's just that he has not been given an official role in the game... until now! The Illusioner at last came out to play in World of Colour. They are nasty mobs, attacking you, or any Villagers and Iron Golems within a 12 block radius. It has a Blindness Spell that will blind you for 20 seconds and can create duplicates of itself to confuse you.

### OPEN THE KNOWLEDGE BOOK

**2** **ARE YOU** always forgetting things? Your homework for school? To make your bed? Your name?! Well you need the Knowledge Book. This handy little green book will tell you the crafting recipes you can use with the stuff you've collected in your inventory. Up until now, the Knowledge Book has been available with the use of Commands in-game, but in the World of Colour update, it plays a much more visible role in the game, helping Minecraft noobs to craft.

# COLOUR

## NEW COLOURED BLOCKS

**3** A RAINBOW of fruity colours came to life in the World of Colour update. Hardened Clay was replaced with Concrete, and it came in 16 super-smooth colours making creating colourful builds a joy! You can now also get Concrete Powder, which falls with gravity. If the Powder comes into contact with Water – you get Concrete. You can also craft Concrete for yourself with 4 Sand, 4 Gravel and any colour of Dye you wish. Just think of the amazing colourful things that can be created with this new block.

## WOOL & BANNER UPDATE

**4** OTHER BLOCKS also had an update, some had new textures, others had changed the way they work. Wool, for example, was given a new texture to make it... well, more Wool-like! This also changed the look of the Sheep! The same with Banners – a new look. Magma Blocks now burn forever, Paintings fill the space they have available, and the underneath of Stairs are now solid, so things like Glass, Torches or Walls can connect to them at last.

## WHO'S A PRETTY BOY THEN?

**5** WHAT BETTER new mob to include for a colourful update like this than Parrots? These delightful birds come in five colours: blue, green, red, light blue and grey and are packed with personality. You can tame them by feeding them Seeds – they will then sit on your shoulder as you walk around, just like a pirate! Don't be tempted to feed them Cookies though – the chocolate chips will kill them and you will get the message "Parrot was slain by *your name*." They jump, they sit and they try to copy the sounds of other mobs around them – cool!

## TIME FOR ADVANCEMENTS

**6** IT'S NOT Achievements any more, it's now Advancements. As you progress through the game you will earn Advancements as you learn new things and there are pop-up messages to reward you. Each section has their own: Minecraft (for the heart of the game), Adventure (for exploration and combat), Husbandry (for crops and friends) then there are ones for The Nether and The End.

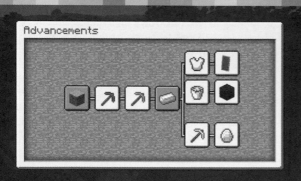

## SAY WHAT YOU SEE...

**7** MINECRAFT CAN be quite intense when you're in the middle of a manic multiplayer game – so now you can choose to have a Narrator speak any chat or in-game messages, leaving you to keep your eyes on the action. Another cool function is you can create 9 custom Saved Toolbars in Creative Mode so you can access the items needed for a mega-build much more quickly.

## SNAZZY TERRACOTTA

**8** WOW LOOK at the swirls on these blocks! This is the Terracotta block, and it comes in 16 colours, each with its own incredible patterns. These blocks can be placed in the world in 4 directions: north, south, east and west, and if you are clever with them, they will build up a picture. The White Terracotta, for example, will build up a picture of a sun. Looking good!

## FUN WITH FUNCTIONS

**10** OKAY, SO functions don't sound like a lot of fun, but it was a brand new system in the World of Colour update that allowed the clever coder people a way of running functions from text files. These are a list of commands for the game that could make just about anything happen. There have been some amazing uses from Functions!

## DYING TO GET TO BED

**9** CONTINUING THE colourful theme, Beds can now be dyed 16 colours, and they have a new 3D model to them, instead of the old 2D shape. That's not all though, you can now bounce on the Beds, which means they can help to save your life if you are falling and there's a handy Bed below. You can in fact survive a 41 block fall onto a bed. Just don't try this in real life!

HOW IS A PHONE LIKE A DIRTY BATH? THEY BOTH HAVE RINGS!

# A SMARTPHONE

## Make a phone that towers over your world!

**EASY**
YOU CAN CONTINUE THE FUN TO MAKE OTHER APP ICONS

**START HERE!**

**1** START BY grabbing Black, Grey, Light Grey, Cyan, Red, and Green Wool blocks and putting them in your hotbar. Next build a circle that's main length is 3 blocks long. Above and below the circle, create the 3 sets of walls as shown (the Light Grey and Grey Wool walls are each 3 blocks in height).

**2** NEXT YOU'LL need to create the telephone, music, email, and battery app icons. Start with the music icon – the right side of this icon should be parallel with the walls from Step 1. Also keep in mind every icon needs a 3 block gap in-between so the phone maintains its shape at the end.

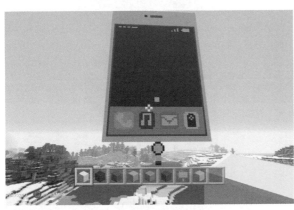

**3** BUILD A massive black slab (around 50 blocks tall!) above the icons and add in the white battery, service and date icons at the top. Then look to the walls above the black circle and begin running them out and around the outside of the phone until you're left with a giant rectangle-like shape.

**4** NOW ALL that's left to do is add in the white upper section with speaker and camera holes, a 3 high White wall below the black circle, and run Grey and Black Wool around the outside. Oh, and be sure to chop the corners off so your phone has that curved shape around the edges.

BUILD THIS!

# MINECRAFT PARTY KIT!

*Why not make your next birthday party a Minecraft party?! Theming the food and decorations is great fun. Here are some food labels to get you started...*

## CUT ALONG THE DOTTED LINES!

**LEAVE MAKING** the actual food to the grown ups – you can have lots of fun cutting out these Minecraft food labels and attaching them to your party plates. We've given you our recommendations for the best type of party food. All we want in return is an invitation!

**WARNING**

ASK MUM, DAD, OR WHOEVER LOOKS AFTER YOU TO HELP WITH SHARP SCISSORS!

Ham
Sandwiches

Carrot
Sticks

Fairy
Cakes

Chocolate
Cookies

Water Melon
Slices

Chicken
Nuggets

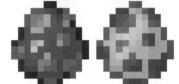

Pizza
Slices

Tuna
Sandwiches

Chocolate
Eggs

Marsh
Mallows

Fish
Fingers

Potato
Crisps

Bottles of
Water

Bread
Sticks

## 5 NEW PARTS

WHILE THE first Story Mode game was 8 parts, this time Telltale Games has returned to their usual 5 parts, with a story that takes Jesse to a creepy underwater temple where he gets his hand stuck in a Prismarine Gauntlet! There are lots of tough choices to make, and with Quicktime Events, you will need to click those buttons with some speed to succeed!

# MINECRAFT
## SEASON TWO
# STORY MODE
### The Telltale Series

*An exciting season of adventures to get stuck into!*

## PUPPY LOVE

WITH RIVALRIES going on between Jesse and his gang, at least he can rely on the love of this cute little puppy dog. Animals feature a lot in the new season of Minecraft: Story Mode, with a very difficult Llama coming along on the new adventure too. But where's Reuben the pig? He was our favourite character! There is also a bunch of familiar faces you will recognise if you've played Season One, and a new scary one – a dark and ancient power that knows Jesse's name – spooky!

## EPISODIC

**TELLTALE GAMES** has specialised in creating what they call 'episodic' adventures. That means that you buy part one, and if you like it you can buy part two, and so on. Once all the parts are released, they are always sold as an all-in-one game, and often at a much lower price too. The first episode of Season Two is called "Hero in Residence" and is on Xbox One, PlayStation 4, PC, Mac, iOS and Android.

## WHO DID YOU UPSET?

**THEY'VE THOUGHT** of everything for the release of Minecraft: Story Mode Season Two. If you've played the first game, all of the decisions you made will carry on through to Season Two, meaning that people you annoyed will still be annoyed with you! But then, brand new players can just jump straight into the action having never played Story Mode before. Here's something cool for multiplayer game fans too – Telltale has a mode called 'Crowd Play'. It means that you and your Minecraft-mad mates can play together from any online mobile device. Cool!

> KEEP THAT STAMPY AWAY FROM ME... I'M ALLERGIC TO CATS!

## FAMOUS CAST

**MANY OF** the actors who did the voices for the first season are back for another go, but most excitingly, there are special guest stars in the game too! YouTube gaming heroes StacyPlays and Stampy Cat have both got parts to play in this game – and you can bet they've made lots of YouTube videos about it!

# KNOW YOUR MINECRAFT MOBS!

One of the most versatile MOBs in Minecraft... you can eat them, keep them in pens and eat their eggs... it's all about eating them really. We give you... the Chicken

ONE OF the most common MOBs in Minecraft, the Chicken naturally spawns in flocks of four on grass blocks. They lay eggs which you can eat for your tea! Strangely, you get more Chickens spawning in jungles than anywhere else! Just like the Pigs, 5% of the Chickens that spawn in the game will be baby Chicks. You also have a one-in-eight chance of getting a baby Chick by throwing eggs around!

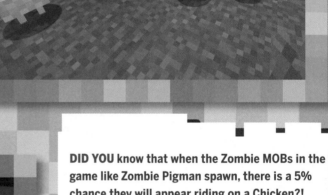

DID YOU know that when the Zombie MOBs in the game like Zombie Pigman spawn, there is a 5% chance they will appear riding on a Chicken?! This is known as a Chicken Jockey! Any MOB spawning as a Chicken Jockey may already be equipped with an item. If you attack the Zombie, they will come after you. Only attack the Chicken they are riding on though, and the Zombie will just leave you alone.

THE ENEMY of the Chicken is the Wild Ocelot. They prefer to stay close to you, and enjoy the company of other farm animals. They are drawn to light areas and don't enjoy the dark. Feed them Wheat, Pumpkin, Melon and Beetroot Seeds and they will love you forever! If you feed these seeds to your Chickens they will breed and make a Baby Chicken. The baby takes 20 minutes to grow!

# PUZZLES

*Test your brains with this teaser...*

## NAME THAT BLOCK

**WHEN YOU** think about it, everything in Minecraft is about blocks. The game just wouldn't run without them! How well do you know your blocks? Now is the time to prove your knowledge...

**1**  `G` `R` `A` `S` `S`

*LOOK! WE'VE DONE THE FIRST ONE FOR YOU!*

**2**

**3**

**4**

**5**

**6**

**7**

ANSWERS ON PAGE 48

*OOO... I DON'T LIKE THE LOOK OF THAT TNT BLOCK, IT MIGHT GO OFF!*

45 MINUTES!

SOME SAY I LOOK A BIT LIKE STONE COLD STEVE AUSTIN!

# WRESTLING RING

## Perfect for multiplayer brawls with your friends!

**DIFFICULTY**

**NORMAL**
QUITE A SIMPLE BUILD, BUT WRESTLING FANS WILL LOVE IT!

**START HERE!**

**1** GRAB YOURSELF some fluffy Black Wool and find a large open area. Next lay down a row of 18 blocks next to one another. Head to the end, turn, and drop down another 18. Do this 2 more times to create a flat, symmetrical square, then build the walls up so they're 2 blocks high.

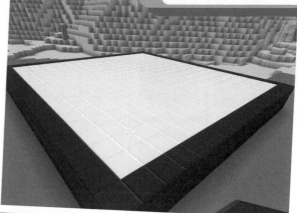

**2** WITH THE base of the ring built it's time to move on to the canvas. Traditionally, canvasses are grey, but Minecraft doesn't really have the right shade of grey, so go with White Wool. For this, just cover the upper-section with White Wool as you won't be able to see the bottom layer.

**3** NEXT, PULL your Black Wool back out. Head to each of the 4 corners and build a spike on them that's 3 blocks tall. These are our turnbuckles, in case that wasn't clear. Turnbuckles are what wrestlers jump off. But don't do that unless you're a wrestler in real life!

**4** WE HAVE two options for the ropes. The first is coloured Carpet, while the second is horizontal End Rods. Basically, Carpet has more colour options, but Rods look more rope-like. If you go with the Carpet, you'll need to build the turnbuckles up by another single block each.

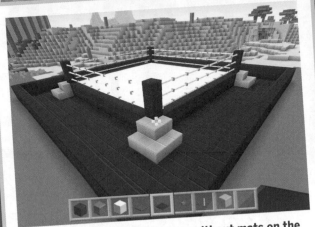

**5** HEAD BACK into the Creative menu and grab some Grey Wool. It's steel steps building time! Go over the top rope and to the outside. At the base of the turnbuckle, lay 1 block either side. Put another block in the middle, then build it up so it resembles a diamond shape.

**6** WHAT'S A wrestling ring without mats on the outside and a guard barricade? Grab some Black Carpet, count 4 blocks out from both sides of the steps and draw an 'L' shape. Continue the square around the outside, fill in the gaps, and build a 2 block high wall around it.

**7** PICK A SIDE of your wrestling ring, any side, and knock out all of that wall except for 4 blocks on each end. Build one side 9 blocks out, make a 2 block high wall for the East side, then create a 4x4 little room on the end that connects back onto the original wall.

**8** GRAB NETHER Steps, a Button, and your Black Wool again. In the small cubicle, the time keeper and announcer's area, lay down 2 Steps to act as seats in front of the two walls. To the left of the chair on the right hand side, add a block of Wool with a Button on top.

BUILD THIS!

HA, HA! IF YOU'RE STONE COLD, I'M THE ROCK!

**9** TO FINISH all we need now is a commentary area. For this, build 2 sets of 2x5 rectangles on the floor. Add Steps on the backside of the second and fourth blocks. Then on the table in front of the chairs, add blocks of Grey Wool with Paintings on to act as monitors. Ready for an epic PvP brawler battle!

# 10 tips for better building in...

# MINECRAFT

**Give your Minecraft builds a boost with these top tips...**

## Tip 1
### QUICK WALLS

**BUILDING A** wall? Don't go from side to side, go up and down instead. The quickest way to create massive structures in Creative mode is to hold down the Place/Use button and Jump button to build upward, and to build in the opposite direction. The game will repeat the process and make it quickly!

GOOD

BAD

## Tip 2
### PERFECT WINDOWS

**WINDOWS ALWAYS** look better with depth. So next time you're adding in a Window frame, try placing the Glass blocks or panes 1 block behind the actual frame. And if you decide to use Panes instead of blocks, it's easier to place the Panes onto already-laid blocks rather than on top of one another.

GOOD

BAD

## Tip 3
### MIX IT UP A BIT

**VARY YOUR** building materials all the time. Using Stone for an entire house is fine, but mixing it up always ends up looking better. Why not use Wood for the roof and Planks for the walls? Have you tried chopping out each corner and replacing it with Wood? Give it a go.

GOOD

BAD

## Tip 4
## POINTY ROOFS

**BUILD ROOFS,** not pyramids. When you've created the main walls of a home, it's easy to think you should run steps all around the outside to create a roof. Don't. You'll end up with a pyramid. Instead, build a step formation going up then build the roof back from there.

GOOD

BAD

## Tip 5
## MAKING TURRETS

**IF YOU'RE** planning on building a castle turret or tower make sure the very bottom, before building it up, has odd-numbered main lengths. If they're even numbers, you won't end up with that lovely spike at the top of the spire when you build it up. This is one of those tips we have found out by trial and error!

GOOD

BAD

DON'T BE A BLOCKHEAD! READ OUR TOP TIPS FOR BETTER MINECRAFT BUILDS!

## Tip 6
## PAPER PLANS

**EVER TRIED** making pixel art from a picture you found online? The reason that works is because you're working from a plan. The same logic applies to everything in Minecraft. Draw some ideas, get a rough idea of size. It doesn't have to look perfect on paper, but it helps to know roughly what you should be doing.

## Tip 7
## GREENERY IS GOOD

**SCENERY IS** as important to your build as block choice. Adding hedges (rows of Leaf blocks), a nice garden, or a mini-farm helps breathe life into your builds. Similarly, pathways help to break up the boring green of the surrounding area. Go on... make your world look great!

# Tips!

YEAH... IT MEANS ONE OF MY FRIENDS IS WALKING AROUND IN HIS SOCKS!

HEY HORSE! DO YOU KNOW WHAT IT MEANS IF YOU FIND A HORSESHOE?

## Tip 8
## TAKE YOUR TIME

**DON'T RUSH.** Seriously, try your hardest not to be impatient. A build that takes 3 hours will always look better than one that's rushed out in 30 minutes. The worst mistake any builder can make is rushing. Rushing leads to mistakes, and mistakes are what you don't want. Enjoy the build experience!

BAD

## Tip 9
## RUN A TEST

**TEST IN** superflat, build in regular worlds. Although clearing out land for a build on pre-made worlds can be time consuming, the surrounding landscape – mountains, ravines, lakes, villages – means your builds will always be surrounded by something. In superflat, the world can seem empty.

GOOD

## Tip 10
## USE YOUR WORLD

**IF YOU'RE** making something big for the first time, consider using your surroundings to help you build. If a castle lookout post seems like it's too difficult, try building it into the side of a mountain. That way you only need to build half, and you've got the option of building rooms inside the mountain.

# FALLING FLOOR TRAP

*Curiosity will kill the cat! Or anyone else who's nosy!*

YOU'RE CAUGHT IN A TRAP! YOU CAN'T WALK OUT! BECAUSE I LOVE YOU TOO MUCH BABY!

**DIFFICULTY**

**EASY**
AS LONG AS YOUR FOES ARE EASILY FOOLED...

START HERE!

**1** BEGIN YOUR nasty scheme by digging up a 3 block wide **trench**. Ours is 7 blocks in length, but you can make it as short or as long as you want. Next, dig the trench downward so you've got a nice big, death-inflicting **drop**. Those nosy enemies won't know what's hit 'em!

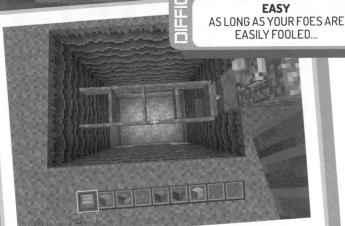

**2** ON THE far side, from ground level, dig 3 blocks down into the wall. Place a **Stone block** in the centre of the gap with a downward-facing **Piston** directly above. Now drop a **block with a Lever**, and place **Signposts** as shown, coming off the Stone. Rub your hands in glee (optional).

**3** YOU SHOULD hopefully be left with a 1 block gap underneath your **Piston** contraption. Now when someone pulls the **Lever**, the block will move and break the **Signpost bridge**. If you want to turn this into a nasty **Lava** trap, add 2 layers of **Lava** at the bottom of the pit.

**4** NOW ALL that's left is to add a falling block, like **Gravel**, above the signs so when the **Piston** breaks the **bridge**, the blocks all fall. To make the trap look less out of place, feel free to drop a **Redstone Lamp** above the **Lever** block and build the **Gravel** out so it looks completely natural.

BUILD THIS!

# Make it!
# CREEPER PUMPKIN!

*Here's an activity that will help you keep your enemies away – make cool Creeper Pumpkins using whatever big fruit or veg you can get!*

## 1 GREEN OR ORANGE?

**FIRST OF ALL**, make sure you have a grown up with you to work on this quick project. Carving a pumpkin is great fun, but knives are sharp and you need to be extra careful! First of all, take your grown up shopping – you need a large green vegetable. You can get green pumpkins these days, or you could try a squash or even a melon. If you can't find anything green, don't worry – the regular orange pumpkin will still look great!

## 2 SCOOP THE GOOP!

**WE'LL ASSUME** you got a pumpkin. Start by having your grown up cut a circular piece out of the top of the pumpkin, around the stalk. This will not only be your lid, but will also give you access to the juicy flesh and seeds within! Lift your 'lid' off and start scooping out the goop. This is the part you can do yourself. Just use a spoon and scoop away until all the goop inside is outside.

## 3 SLICE & DICE!

**NOW IT'S** time to carve the Creeper's face. You all know what a Creeper's face looks like, right? Just in case, take a look at our carving here. It's basically made up of 2 big squares carved to make the eyes. Then 3 rectangles for the nose and fangs. Have your grown up slowly slice through the pumpkin from the outside in, being careful not to overcut each line, making up the shapes. With a piece cut, push out from the inside and it will 'pop' out! Continue around the face until the full Creeper look has taken shape.

## 4 LIGHTS!

**GREAT WORK!** Now all you need to do is put some kind of light inside your Creeper pumpkin's head. You can get some great battery operated 'candles' these days that will make it really safe to use, or if you want the authentic Halloween feel, have your grown up light some tea light candles and place them inside the Creeper pumpkin – hey presto! A super scary Creeper that will keep those evil spirits away from your door!

# PUZZLES

## Test your brains with this teaser...

## FOOD SUDOKU

**HAVE YOU** tried a **Sudoku**? It's a tricky puzzle where you must make sure that **each line of 4**, top to bottom and left to right, **has only one of each item**. Oh, and each block of 4 also has to have only one of each item too. See if you can **draw in the missing food**...

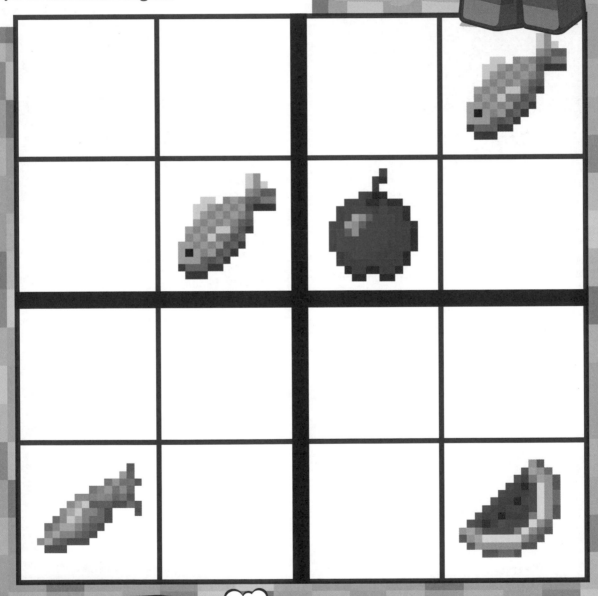

YUM, YUM! I'M GOING TO HAVE A FEAST WHEN YOU'RE DONE!

ANSWERS ON PAGE 48

# Build It!

## 60 MINUTES!

GROUND FLOOR: PERFUMERY, STATIONERY, AND LEATHER GOODS...

# REDSTONE LIFT

### Going up! Make a working lift for your next build!

**DIFFICULTY**

**HARD**
REDSTONE IS TRICKY STUFF, FOLLOW THE STEPS CAREFULLY

**START HERE!**

**1** THERE ARE various ways you can build a lift in Minecraft. We've chosen one we think everyone can have a go at! Start by breaking a hole in the ground and placing a **Normal Piston** facing up in it. This will be the front of your lift. Place your favourite colour of **Concrete** next to your Piston, then a second **Piston** to the right of that block facing upwards.

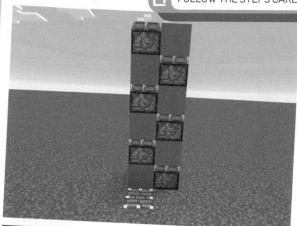

**2** YOU NEED to repeat this process of blocks and Pistons alternating as many times as you want going up. As you can see above, we chose to repeat the pattern **6 times**. What is going to happen is that these Pistons are going to be pushed out by other Pistons we are going to place in a moment.

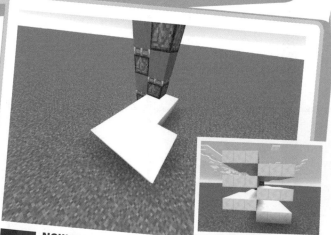

**3** NOW IT'S time to build the foundations where the Redstone is going to run. Grab some **Quartz** blocks and head to the back of your lift. Place **4 Quartz** blocks going back from your first Concrete block, then **5 Quartz** blocks alongside this line, and finally **2 Quartz** blocks alongside that – take a look above for placement. Repeat this process, flipping the pattern, as you go up – look at the small picture.

**4** AS WE said earlier, we need more Pistons to push the Pistons we already placed! Get **Sticky Pistons** this time, and place them behind the Normal Pistons, facing into them. Repeat this again on every Normal Piston in the build, except for the very first one we put in the ground. What we are doing here is setting up a reaction that we will control with Redstone to activate the lift!

**5** NOW PLACE a pillar of Concrete in your chosen colour on the front of either side of your build. This is so people will not fall out of the lift when going up! Next go to each side of the lift and cover up each Sticky Piston with a Concrete block. We do this to carry Redstone current through the lift to power the Pistons.

**6** NOW GO to the back of your lift. Place 2 Redstone Repeaters facing into the Concrete block and Sticky Piston. We now have to change the Ticks on one of the Repeaters, but be careful as if you change the wrong Repeater, the entire lift will malfunction! The Repeater facing the Sticky Piston must be 3 Ticks, do this by clicking it 3 times. Repeat this all the way up your lift as before.

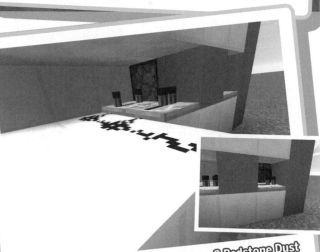

**7** REDSTONE DUST time! Place 3 Redstone Dust on top of the Quartz blocks next to the Repeaters and continue the path of the Dust to the right as shown in the picture. In the gap shown in the small picture above, place another Repeater facing the front of the lift. Again, repeat this all the way up.

**8** ON THE left side of your lift dig a 5 block long trench that ends 1 block in front of the Concrete pillar. Now extend this trench backwards by 2 blocks, underneath the Quartz. Dig 2 more blocks out on the right, under the Quartz block – take a look at the small picture to see how your trench should end up.

**9** STICK SOME Redstone Repeaters into the extending holes you just made in the trench, they must be facing into the end blocks of each hole so that they link the Redstone. Set the left-hand Repeater shown above to 1 Tick by clicking it once. Lay Redstone Dust along the trench to link everything up. Break the block under the Concrete pillar and place some Redstone Dust there too.

**10** NOW IT'S time to place a Button that will activate your lift. Put down a Quartz block and Concrete block combo, then place a Stone Button on the Concrete in a handy place! Link the star of the Redstone in your trench to the Stone Button with more Redstone Dust. Once the button is pressed signal will travel through the lift!

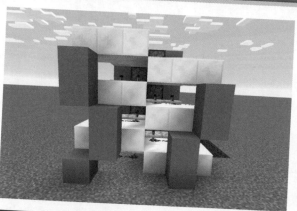

**11** USING CONCRETE blocks, go to the back of your lift and copy the pattern shown above in our snazzy Cyan Concrete blocks. We are setting the lift up to carry the signal of the Redstone from the Redstone Repeaters into Redstone Dust on the level above.

**12** WE NOW need to place Redstone Repeaters facing into the Concrete pattern we just made. Each level of your lift will have a Concrete block to attach to. Place a single Repeater on each level and set it to 1 Tick by clicking it once. This is an easy way to carry the Redstone signal around.

**13** AT THE end of your trench where there are two Quartz blocks, place some Redstone Dust on the last Quartz block and the grass below, completing your Redstone Dust circuits. This will link the Button you placed with the Pistons around the lift.

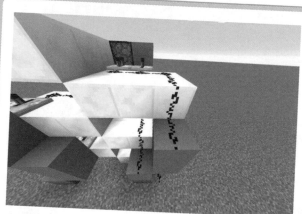

**14** PLACE REDSTONE Dust on top of the coloured Concrete blocks at the back of your lift. This allows the power to travel from level to level in your lift easily. Make sure that the Redstone is all connected up by whizzing around your lift to check.

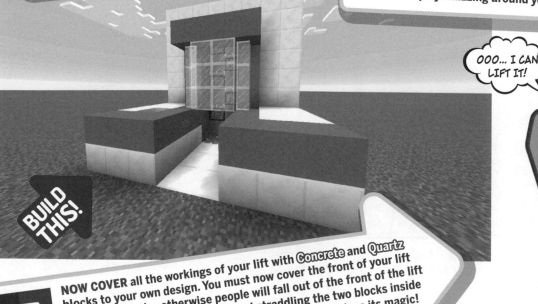

**BUILD THIS!**

OOO... I CAN LIFT IT!

**15** NOW COVER all the workings of your lift with Concrete and Quartz blocks to your own design. You must now cover the front of your lift with Glass blocks, otherwise people will fall out of the front of the lift when going up! To use the lift, stand straddling the two blocks inside and press the Button! Hold on tight as the Redstone does its magic!

# KNOW YOUR MINECRAFT MOBS!

Minecraft MOBs don't just come in friendly living variations you know! There is also a bunch of undead ones, like... Zombies!

**THE ZOMBIES** like to come out when it's dark. They spawn in groups of four when the light level is seven or less. In places like Deserts where the sun is baking down, Zombies will turn into burnt out Husks 80% of the time. There are also Zombie Villager types with big noses and Baby Zombies that will pop up from time to time. There's a 5% chance the babies will be riding a Chicken and make a Chicken Jockey!

**WATCH OUT** around your villages at night-time. If your village has at least ten doors and 20 villagers, then the Zombies will come out to play! Up to 20 Zombies can be spawned at the edge of your village, no matter which biome you build it in. If you find yourself in a Dungeon, watch out as Zombies will spawn from Monster Spawners found in the centre of the Dungeon 50% of the time. The rest of the time it will be Skeletons and Spiders.

**THESE ZOMBIES** aren't the dumb kind you know! If they come across dropped items, they will pick them up and use them against you! This can create some tricky situations where a Zombie can have full Golden Armour and a dangerous Sword. You can always put another rubbish item in front of them to stop the danger – they are stupid enough to drop their Sword and pick up your new item.

# KNOW YOUR MINECRAFT BLOCKS!

The secret to success in Minecraft is knowing which block does what Let us tell you all about *Diamonds!*

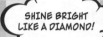

SHINE BRIGHT LIKE A DIAMOND!

**1** The easiest place to find Diamonds is near lava, but you'll need either a Diamond or Iron Pickaxe to mine it.

**2** According to spawn rates, the highest chance of finding Diamonds is in End City and Nether Fortress Chests.

**3** Enchanting a Pickaxe with Fortune means you'll get even more Diamonds per vein.

**4** While Diamond has the best durability, Gold still offers higher damage, mining speed and protection.

**5** The maximum amount of Diamonds you will be able to find in one set of ore is up to 12.

**6** When Diamonds were first added to Minecraft, they were referred to as 'emeralds'. Imagine that?!

**7** Always dig around Diamond Ore in case a second set has spawned nearby, and also to prevent them from falling in Lava.

**8** Throwing a Diamond at another player results in unlocking the achievement 'Diamonds to You'.

**9** In Minecraft: Pocket Edition, Diamonds were used to create the now-removed Nether Reactor core block.

**10** It takes 9 Diamonds to create a Diamond block, meaning it would take 675 Diamonds in total to build the smallest villager house.

# PUZZLES

## Test your brains with this teaser...

THIS PUZZLE MAKES MY ZOMBIE BRAIN HURT!

## A TRICKY RIVER CROSSING

**STEVE HAS** to get a Wolf, a Chicken and a loaf of Bread from one side of the river to the other. He has crafted a Boat, but it's only big enough to carry himself and one other thing. The problem is that if the Wolf and Chicken are left behind, the Wolf will eat the Chicken. If the Chicken and Bread are left together there will be no Bread left when Steve returns. How can he get all three of them to the other side of the river?

ANSWERS ON PAGE 48

**20** MINUTES!

WHERE IS THE SECRET ENTRANCE? IF I TOLD YOU, IT WOULDN'T BE SECRET!

# A SECRET WALL

## A secret wall entrance may come in very handy!

DIFFICULTY

**NORMAL**
QUITE A SIMPLE BUILD, BUT MAY BE VERY USEFUL...

**START HERE!**

**1** FIRST THINGS first, pull out some Stone and Sticky Pistons. Lay down six Stone blocks all in a long row and knock out the middle two blocks. Next, on the left side, create an 'L' shape out of Sticky Pistons. After that, head to the right and do the same but in reverse.

**2** PLACE YOUR wall blocks in front of the Sticky Pistons. We're using Gold blocks here to show you where they should go, but If your wall is going to be made of Stone, use Stone blocks instead. After that, run a row of Stone blocks across the top-front to create an archway.

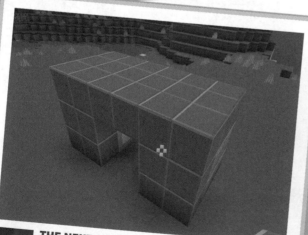

**3** THE NEXT thing we need to do is build a roof on top of our device so we can lay down Redstone. Coming from the row above the doorframe, add in another 2 rows behind it. You can now go ahead and add Redstone Repeaters and Redstone Dust to your hotbar.

**4** ONE BLOCK in from both sides place down Redstone Repeaters facing outward. This next part is important: Hit each of them once so they're both on 2 ticks. If you don't, the wall will push the wrong parts out. Next dust in the Redstone in between and around, as shown.

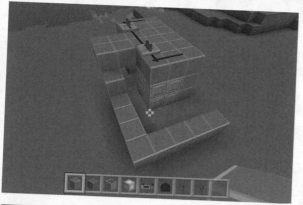

**5** NOW IT'S time to add in somewhere for our Lever to go. Add in 4 blocks behind the Redstone Dust. Next add a Step down, build it 4 blocks out, then 4 to the right. Do not build the arm too close to the Pistons as it'll accidentally activate them, and we really don't want that.

**6** LOOKING FROM the back, connect the Redstone Dust on the right (in between the Repeaters) down and along the stone arm. One block after the steps, drop in a Repeater facing the steps. At the end of the arm add another block with a Lever on its face.

**7** GO ON, you know you want to. Pull the Lever and marvel at our really simple, really compact, Redstone secret wall. If you're looking to add a Lever on the inside, place one on the back of the step you made leading to the lever. That way you can close the wall behind you.

**8** IF YOU'RE creating this out in the open, now's a good time to build up the walls around it. Do keep in mind you don't want to place blocks directly on top of the Redstone as it will disrupt the circuit. So be sure to build the walls a few blocks taller to avoid any issues.

**BUILD THIS!**

**9** YOUR SECRET wall can be placed anywhere, and can lead to whatever you want. Why not try building a library with a hidden bookcase entrance to a loot room? Or why stop at a loot room? Build the door into a mountain then you'll have the space to create an entire house behind it!

> I READ A BOOK ONCE. GREEN, IT WAS.

# DOUBLE AQUATIC WORDSEARCH

## Find all the Aquatic update words and the secret names!

### WHO'S HIDING?

**THE NEW** Aquatic update for Minecraft is packed with watery words, and we've crammed 42 of them into these two wordsearches. Find all the words, ticking them off as you go, then unscramble the highlighted letters to find out the two heroes hiding in the puzzle!

*WHEN YOU FIND A WORD, USE A COLOURED PEN TO DRAW A LINE THROUGH IT!*

### WORDS TO FIND...

- [ ] AQUATIC
- [ ] BEDROCK
- [ ] CONDUIT
- [ ] CORAL
- [ ] DEEPSEA
- [ ] DOLPHIN
- [ ] DROWNED
- [ ] FISH
- [ ] KELP
- [ ] MARINE
- [ ] MINECRAFT
- [ ] MYTHICAL
- [ ] OCEAN
- [ ] PHANTOM
- [ ] REEF
- [ ] RUINS
- [ ] SEAGRASS
- [ ] SEAPICKLE
- [ ] SHIPWRECK
- [ ] TRAPDOOR
- [ ] TREASURE
- [ ] TRIDENT
- [ ] TURTLE

| D | O | L | P | H | I | N | E | C | I | W | C |
|---|---|---|---|---|---|---|---|---|---|---|---|
| B | E | D | R | O | C | K | L | U | A | I | Y |
| R | S | N | I | U | R | O | T | G | T | H | O |
| S | O | M | I | N | E | C | R | A | F | T | S |
| S | P | O | B | D | R | Q | U | A | R | X | E |
| A | H | L | D | E | R | Q | T | E | L | D | W |
| R | A | I | E | P | A | O | A | A | E | X | P |
| G | N | F | P | K | A | S | W | E | Y | T | T |
| A | T | I | B | W | U | R | P | N | K | I | C |
| E | O | S | U | R | R | S | T | G | E | U | K |
| S | M | H | E | G | E | E | J | O | O | D | L |
| E | N | I | R | A | M | O | C | E | A | N | O |
| L | A | C | I | H | T | Y | M | K | Y | O | Z |
| T | N | E | D | I | R | T | W | A | K | C | E |

**WHAT DID THE SEA SAY TO THE BEACH?**

**NOTHING... IT JUST WAVED!**

## WORDS TO FIND...

- ☐ BLUEICE
- ☐ BUBBLE
- ☐ BUCKET
- ☐ CHANNELING
- ☐ COD
- ☐ DEEPOCEAN
- ☐ HEARTOFTHESEA
- ☐ IMPALING
- ☐ LOYALTY
- ☐ MAP
- ☐ MEMBRANE
- ☐ NAUTILUSSHELL
- ☐ PRISMARINE
- ☐ PUFFERFISH
- ☐ RIPTIDE
- ☐ SALMON
- ☐ SCUTE
- ☐ TROPICAL
- ☐ WARM

| M | E | H | X | L | L | I | C | O | D | T | P |
|---|---|---|---|---|---|---|---|---|---|---|---|
| O | T | E | E | L | A | M | X | H | E | R | U |
| T | U | A | D | E | C | P | E | G | E | I | F |
| N | C | R | I | H | I | A | C | N | P | D | F |
| A | S | T | T | S | P | L | I | I | O | E | E |
| H | L | O | P | S | O | I | E | L | C | N | R |
| P | O | F | I | U | R | N | U | E | E | T | F |
| S | Y | T | R | L | T | G | L | N | A | P | I |
| A | A | H | H | I | V | B | B | N | N | A | S |
| L | L | E | I | T | B | M | R | A | W | M | H |
| M | T | S | G | U | F | I | S | H | E | L | L |
| O | Y | E | B | A | T | E | K | C | U | B | O |
| N | X | A | E | N | A | R | B | M | E | M | S |
| P | R | I | S | M | A | R | I | N | E | V | H |

**THE MYSTERY HEROES ARE...**

☐ ☐ ☐ ☐

☐ ☐ ☐ ☐ ☐

ANSWERS ON PAGE 48

## DIFFICULTY

★★★

**HARD**
BUT WORTH EVERY SECOND
SPENT GETTING IT RIGHT!

## INFO

**GHOST TRAIN**

**TIME NEEDED:** 1 HOUR
**EXTRA INFO:** WHO'S GOING TO
RIDE YOUR GHOST TRAIN? PUT
IN WHAT WILL SCARE THEM

# BUILD A SPOOKY...
# GHOST TRAIN

## Want to scare your Minecraft mates? Make this ghoulish train ride!

*I'VE GOT A SPOOKY PARTY INVITE, BUT I'VE GOT NO BODY TO GO WITH!*

**60 MINUTES!**

**HERE IS** a fun build that you can use to scare your friends when you have a Minecraft play date – a terrifying fairground ride! This is a bit of a challenge, but once you get this adapted minecart ride working, you'll be glad you took the time. You can experiment with adding your own personal nightmares to the creepiness within! Let's get started... hold someone's hand if you're too scared to do it on your own!

## 1

### IN THE BEGINNING

**TO KEEP** a Minecart moving, you need to use a Powered Rail, which needs a Redstone Torch nearby to power it. Another thing to keep in mind, don't use Powered Rails or Detector Rails on corners. They won't work and your cart could just stop.

## 2

### ATOP THE MOUNTAIN

**GRAB RED,** White and Black Wool, Redstone blocks, and White and Red Terracotta. Start by dropping a row of 8 Red Wool for the bottom lip. From here, add in Black and White for the mouth. Add an upper-lip, then fill in the skin with Terracotta.

## 3

### BRAIN DEAD

**NOW ADD** in the White sides and continue the mouth. Drop in the hair on both sides with Red Wool then grab end blocks and end bricks for the creepy brain on top. For the back of the head, fill in with White Terracotta. Fingers are optional!

## 4

### NOW THE TRACK

**KNOCK OUT** 2 blocks vertically from the face. Head on into the creative menu and equip Nether Brick. Now build a staircase from the mouth to ground level. Add Rails and Powered Rails and give it a quick test to see if it works.

## 5

### MORE TRACK

**IF YOUR** Minecart made it all the way up you're safe to move on to building more track. Mine through the head to the other side. Run a row of tracks and then build the track upwards at the end. Continue around to the right by around 10 blocks.

## 6

### RIDE THE TRACK

**TAKE A** ride and see where the cart falls. There, place 4 tracks behind the point of impact and work your way forwards. Continue down the mountainside and around to the front with the intention of building into the front of the mountain.

## 7

### GHASTLY!

**DIG A** 2 high, 7 long cave. Turn the end of the corridor into a 5 wide room. Add in rows of Dispensers on both sides, then dig a trench below the Dispensers. Add Stone above the Dispensers, place Detector Rails in the middle then fill with Ghasts!

## 8

### ZOMBIE JUMP SCARE

**DIG OUT** a 3x3 hole 4 blocks deep. In the centre, dig a block and place an upward-facing Sticky Piston. Lay a block on top, then Soul Sand. Finally, drop an Armour Stand on top of that and watch as it mysteriously sinks.

**9**

## SPOOKY NIGHT

**ADD ARMOUR** and a head. Place Soul Sand on top, then place a Piston facing down above that. Next grab Redstone and place it next to that. What should happen is the Soul Sand is pushed into the Armour Stand. Now remove the Piston and Redstone.

**10**

## GRAVE ERROR

**IN FRONT**, on the ground, drop Redstone Dust. Trail it on to a step then up and under where your track will go. Use a Lever to test it, and if it works, change the Lever for a Detector Rail. Finish off with Grass, Coal, and Half Slabs for tombtones.

**11**

## ZOMBIE SCARES

**MAKE SURE** you have a 4 block gap between zombie scares, and don't forget to place the Detector Rails on top of the final Redstone Dust. If you used these in another build, substitute the Detector Rail for a Pressure Plate and they'll work.

**12**

## LAVA-LY STUFF

**CONTINUE THE** track along by digging a 2 high corridor. Mine up the walls then dig a 1 block trench – floor and ceiling. At the end of the corridor, create a Step leading up. Now go back to the 2 trenches and fill them with Lava!

**13**

## SLIME TIME

**CONTINUE UP** from the Step to ground level. Add a corner turn at the top so the track leads out to the left. At the end add Slime with an upward facing Piston below. Place Redstone below and trail it to a Detector block. The Minecart will jump on Slime!

**14**

## MORE TRACK

**WHERE THE** Minecart lands, place Nether Bricks with a Rail on. Add a straight then a big climb. Drop in another straight, a turn, and then one more straight. Deck it out with powered rails and, like always, give it a test run.

## 15

### GOING UNDERGROUND

**HAVING BUILT** the track high, let the **Minecart** ride off and where it lands, dig a 3 wide hole 15 blocks deep. Make sure you put **rail** just in front in case your cart doesn't land flush. Now comes an eerie hallway that's sunken into the earth.

## 16

### THE SECRET ROOM

**A FIVE** wide hallway next. Replace walls with **Quartz** blocks (**Half Slabs** for the ceiling). Change floor for planks and hang **Paintings**. Create 2 tables, add a **Sea Lantern** to the ceiling and make a 2 high **Window** in the centre of the end wall.

## 17

### MORE OF THE SAME

**AROUND THE** corner create another small room on the right. There's a lot of repetition to go through here, just to ensure your Ghost Train is full of detail. Add another **Armour Stand** (with **Armour** and a **Head**) and place a door in front of it.

## INSPIRATION

**HALLOWEEN MINE CART** TheGeekBarbie showed off an epic creation on YouTube.

**MINECRAFT GHOST TRAIN** Great job by David Crotty Nangle on his spooky train!

**MAD HOUSE** Tom Weller took a slightly different scary route, see it on YouTube!

## 18

### DOOR SLAM

**IN THE** centre of the hallway outside, dig down and lay **Redstone Dust** that leads to a **Redstone Torch** directly under the door. Add a **Pressure Plate** to test and the door should slam shut when you approach it.

# Build It!

## 19

### ANOTHER CORRIDOR

> PLACE 2 **Crafting Tables** with a **Redstone Torch** on top then turn to the left and create a front door area. Add an **ArmourStand** to the right to look like a coat rack then a plant on the left. All this is to lure the rider into a false sense of security!

## 20

### SCREAM FOR SPEED

> AT THE end of the corridor dig a 4 block long trench. Place 3 downward facing **Dispensers** and fill with **Ghasts**. Now place **TNT** around the **Dispensers**, cover over with **Wood**, lay in **Detector Rails** and this ride is sure to end with a **bang**!

THERE'S NO GHOST TRAIN THAT CAN SCARE A SPIDER JOCKEY!

# KNOW YOUR MINECRAFT MOBS!

'MOB' is short for 'Mobile' you know?! It's a quick way of referring to any character in the game. Let's check out the *Villagers*

IF YOU make a Village they will come! Villagers spawn in villages built in biomes like Deserts, Savannas, Forests, Taigas and Plains. There are six types of Villager, and they are all friendly, passive MOBs that you can Trade with. There's the farmer, librarian, priest, nitwit, butcher and blacksmith – but within these trades there are also variations like armourer, cartographer and shepherd. They bring the place to life!

THE ZOMBIES are back! If a Zombie kills a Villager, it will return as a Zombie Villager – just like in scary movies! There's also another MOB called an Illager – these are hostile and spawn in outposts or woodland mansions. It is thought that they are outcasts from Villages who are out to seek revenge! They will attack you as soon as look at you, and they will also pick fights with the good Villagers and Iron Golems!

YOU CAN trade Emeralds for other items with Villagers, and the trade can be good or bad – it's kind of potluck! Trading is the best way of getting rare items like Chain Armour though, so it's always worth seeing what the Villagers you encounter have to offer. When a Villager has a new trade to offer, they will have pink and green haze appearing around them – have a chat to find out what it is!

# MAKE A MOB MASK!

**WARNING**

ASK MUM, DAD, OR WHOEVER LOOKS AFTER YOU TO HELP WITH SHARP SCISSORS!

*Get your colouring pens out because we've got a fun Minecraft activity that will need them! Make yourself a MOB mask! Follow the coloured pixels of your favourite MOB below, copying them into the giant grid. Then cut it out, add some elastic between the holes and wear your MOB!*

# PUZZLE ANSWERS

## PAGE 10
### AQUATIC SPOT THE DIFFERENCE
Check out the 10 differences in the picture...

## PAGE 21
### NAME THAT BLOCK
The blocks were:
1. Grass
2. Glowstone
3. Jack O'Lantern
4. Hay Bale
5. Crafting Table
6. Spawner
7. TNT

## PAGE 29
### FOOD SUDOKU
This is where all the food items go...

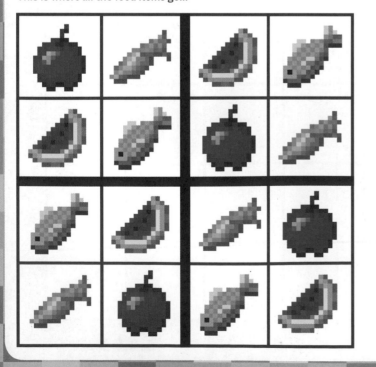

## PAGE 35
### A TRICKY RIVER CROSSING
Steve must first take the Chicken across the river as the Wolf and the Bread are safe together. He must leave the Chicken on the other side and go back across. Now the Wolf gets to ride in the boat, but Steve must bring the Chicken back with him, as it will become a snack for the Wolf if left together. He must leave the Chicken on the other side, bringing the Bread across this time, leaving it with the Wolf. Now, finally Steve can cross the river, pick up the Chicken and end up with all three of them on the other side of the river.

## PAGE 38
### DOUBLE AQUATIC WORDSEARCH
Here is where all the words are hidden...

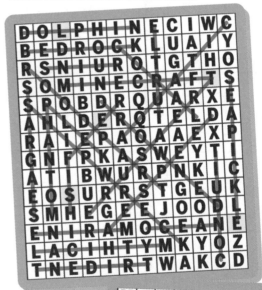

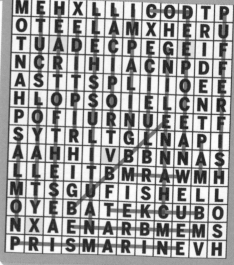

The mystery heroes were STEVE and ALEX.